Too Bad, Ahab

NABOTH'S VINEYARD

By Marilyn Lashbrook

Illustrated by Chris Sharp

CANDLE
BOOKS

ME TOO! READERS are designed
to help you share the joy of reading
with children. They provide a new
and fun way to improve a child's
reading skills- by practice and
example. At the same time, you are
teaching your child valuable Bible
truths.

TOO BAD, AHAB! is a story that
every child can relate to. It opens up
a wide range of topics for discussion:
pouting and selfishness, God's
mercy and fairness, obedience and
the value of contentment.

Reading is key to successful
education. Obeying the principles of
God's Word opens the door to a
successful life. ME TOO! READERS
encourage your children in both!

Bold type: Child reads
Regular type: Adult reads

First published in the UK by Candle Books Ltd. 1995.
Distributed by STL., P.O. Box 300,
Carlisle, Cumbria CA3 0JH.

Coedition arranged by Angus Hudson Ltd., London.

Printed in Italy.

ISBN 1 85985 037 5

Too Bad, Ahab

NABOTH'S VINEYARD

By Marilyn Lashbrook

Illustrated by Chris Sharp

Taken from 1 Kings 21

Naboth had the worst neighbours anyone ever had. They were the devilish pair, King Ahab and Queen Jezebel. Ahab and Jezebel lived in a palace right next door to Naboth.

Naboth owned a beautiful vineyard. Mountain streams carried water and rich top soil to his land. Naboth took pride in growing the finest of grapes.

A grape vineyard is a special kind of garden. The vines can live more than a hundred years. Some of the vines in Naboth's vineyard may have been planted by his great-grandfather.

"One day," Naboth thought, I will give this land to my sons." That was Naboth's dream.

But someone else was dreaming about Naboth's vineyard, too.

That somebody was his nasty neighbour, King Ahab.

Ahab saw the strong, healthy vines in Naboth's vineyard. He looked at the huge clusters of sweet, juicy grapes hanging from the vines. He thought about the kinds of plants he would grow if he owned Naboth's land.

"Let's see now, maybe some
big, red tomatoes,
and some sweet potatoes.
A tree full of cherries,
and a patch for strawberries
I'll grow some carrots,
and cabbage,
and corn on the cob,
and cucumbers for pickles
to eat with hot dogs.

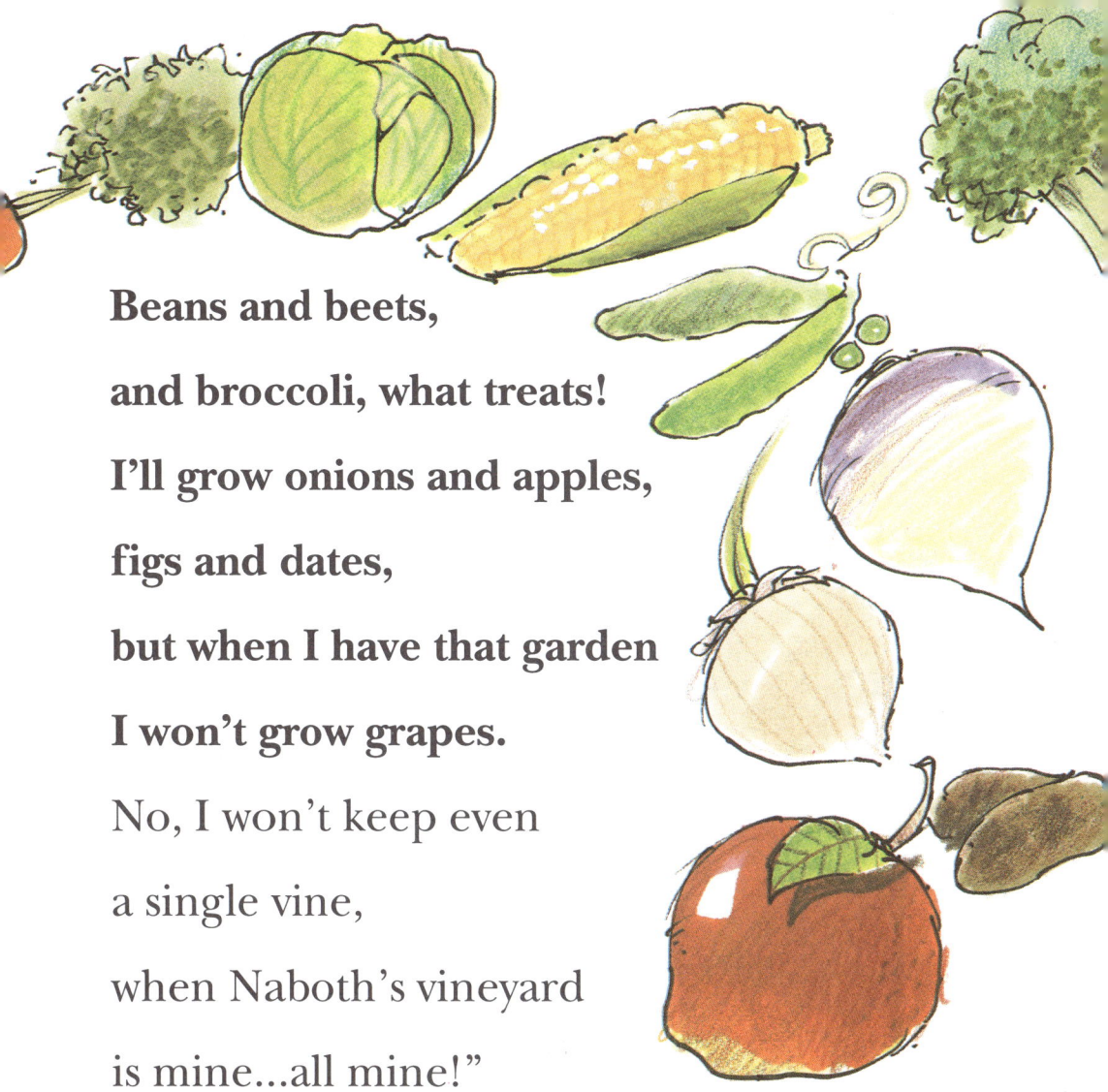

Beans and beets,

and broccoli, what treats!

I'll grow onions and apples,

figs and dates,

but when I have that garden

I won't grow grapes.

No, I won't keep even

a single vine,

when Naboth's vineyard

is mine...all mine!"

The longer Ahab thought about it, the more he coveted that vineyard! Do you think we should get every thing we want?

Too bad, Ahab! You have so much. You should be glad.

One day, Ahab went to talk to Naboth.

"I want to buy your vineyard," Ahab said. "It is close to my palace, and I want it for a vegetable garden."

Naboth was horrified! He couldn't imagine someone digging up his precious vines and tossing them in a trash heap.

"No!" said Naboth, "God told us not to sell the land of our fathers.

Naboth chose to obey God and to keep the land for his children and their children's children.

Too bad, Ahab!

Don't be mad.

Ahab sighed and slouched and stuck out his lower lip. Then he went home feeling angry and depressed. And he flopped on his bed and pouted like a spoiled child. He even refused to eat!

God had warned his people not to covet anything belonging to a neighbour. But as usual, Ahab chose to disobey God. Soon, Ahab's selfishness and sulking got him into big trouble.

Too bad, Ahab!

Stop acting so sad.

Queen Jezebel waltzed into Ahab's room. "Why are you pouting? she asked, "Why don't you eat?"

Ahab did not even turn over. "Because," he whined, "I asked Naboth to sell me his vineyard and he said 'no!'"

Jezebel was disgusted with her husband. "Cheer up!" she said, "I'll get you your vineyard."

Ahab knew Jezebel had killed people before, and he knew she was not afraid to kill again. Ahab didn't care. He wanted that vineyard and it didn't matter to him if he had to lie, steal, and kill to get it.

Jezebel wrote some letters and put Ahab's stamp on them. Then she sent the letters to the rulers of the city.

The rulers followed Jezebel's orders and called all the people in the town to fast and pray. They seated Naboth in front of everyone.

Then two lying rascals pointed to Naboth. In loud voices, they said, "This man cursed God! We heard him curse God and the king."

"That isn't true!" Naboth shouted. He was frantic. He knew the punishment for cursing God was death. What could he do?

How could he prove he was not guilty? The rulers would not listen to Naboth's pleading. "Take him out and kill him!" they said.

And the people dragged Naboth away and put him to death.

When Ahab heard Naboth was dead, he jumped out of bed and ran to take the vineyard for himself. But his excitement did not last long.

God was very angry. King Ahab was more evil than any man who ever lived. So God sent His prophet to take a message to Ahab. What do you think Ahab's punishment should be?

Elijah, God's prophet, went to Naboth's vineyard. That's where he found the selfish king.

Ahab knew he was guilty. But he did not want to admit he had sinned. "So you have found me, my enemy!" Ahab sneered.

"I have found you," Elijah said, "because you do nothing but disobey God's laws. You have murdered a man and you too must die.

When Ahab heard that, he hung his head and was quiet before God. And God saw him and had pity on Ahab.

Because God is more loving then any person, He was merciful to Ahab. "I will wait awhile before bringing this punishment."

God is merciful, but He is also fair. He always keeps His word.

So a few years later, at the very place where Naboth was killed, Ahab died in a battle. Ahab killed Naboth to take his vineyard. But Ahab paid for the vineyard with his own life.

Too bad, Ahab!

You should have been happy with what you had.

ME TOO!
B O O K S

For Ages 2-5

SOMEONE TO LOVE
THE STORY OF CREATION

TWO BY TWO
THE STORY OF NOAH'S FAITH

"I DON'T WANT TO"
THE STORY OF JONAH

"I MAY BE LITTLE"
THE STORY OF DAVID'S GROWTH

"I'LL PRAY ANYWAY"
THE STORY OF DANIEL

WHO NEEDS A BOAT?
THE STORY OF MOSES

"GET LOST LITTLE BROTHER"
THE STORY OF JOSEPH

THE WALL THAT DID NOT FALL
THE STORY OF RAHAB'S FAITH

NO TREE FOR CHRISTMAS
THE STORY OF JESUS' BIRTH

"NOW I SEE"
THE STORY OF THE MAN BORN BLIND

DON'T ROCK THE BOAT!
THE STORY OF THE MIRACULOUS CATCH

OUT ON A LIMB
THE STORY OF ZACCHAEUS

ME TOO!
R E A D E R S

For Ages 5-8

IT'S NOT MY FAULT
MAN'S BIG MISTAKE

GOD, PLEASE SEND FIRE!
ELIJAH AND THE PROPHETS OF BAAL

TOO BAD, AHAB!
NABOTH'S VINEYARD

THE WEAK STRONGMAN
SAMSON

NOTHING TO FEAR
JESUS WALKS ON WATER

THE BEST DAY EVER
THE STORY OF JESUS

THE GREAT SHAKE-UP
MIRACLES IN PHILIPPI

TWO LADS AND A DAD
THE PRODIGAL SON